God
Idea vs. Good Idea

Spirit or Soul

Kevin L. Cann

Litchfield, IL 62056

© 2014 by Kevin Cann

All rights reserved. No part of this book may be reproduced, stored in a retrieval system or transmitted in any form or by any means without the prior written permission of the publishers, except by a reviewer who may quote brief passages in a review to be printed in a newspaper, magazine or journal.

1st Printing

Publisher has allowed this work to remain exactly as the author intended, verbatim, without editorial input.

Unless otherwise indicated, all Scripture quotations are taken from *The Holy Bible, New King James Version.* Copyright © 1979, 1980, 1982 by Thomas Nelson, Inc.

EBook 978-1-304-94874-8

Softcover 978-1-304-94870-0

Hardcover 978-1-304-94872-4

PUBLISHED BY REVIVAL WAVES OF GLORY BOOKS & PUBLISHING
www.revivalwavesofglory.com
Litchfield, IL
Printed in the United States of America

Table of Contents

Dedication 5
Introduction 7
Chapter 1 Relationships 9
Chapter 2 Business 17
Chapter 3 Investing 27
Chapter 4 Ministry 33
Chapter 5 Soul 37
Chapter 6 Spirit 41
Chapter 7 Prophecy 45
Chapter 8 Divine Council 51
God Idea or Good Idea Evaluation Sheet 57
Contact the Author 59
Other Books Available 61

DEDICATION

I would like to dedicate this book to my Heavenly Father. He gave me the words to put in this book. This book would not be possible without the help of the Holy Spirit giving me guidance and direction. I am thankful to Jesus Christ for saving me from my sins. I thank all three from the bottom of my heart.

I would also like to dedicate this book to my beautiful wife, Bethany. She has helped me get out of my comfort zone and become a finisher. I love you.

INTRODUCTION

I have had a lot of good ideas over the years. I have tried to be successful with all kinds of different ideas. My good ideas are just that: good ideas. When I began to write this book it was only two weeks after I had finished my first book: "Who is Your $ource". My first book was definitely a God idea, not one of *my* good ideas. This book is not one of my good ideas, either. I am not a natural born author. I have to rely on the Holy Spirit to give me words for a book. As I am writing this right now, the Holy Spirit is giving me the words to write. I even put my computer down but the words kept coming to me from the Holy Spirit. This is how we know it's a *God idea* and not a *good idea*. We are all looking for good ideas. It doesn't matter if we are in relationships, business, ministry, etc, but our destiny is full of *God ideas*. The difficult part is trying to separate the *God idea* from the *good ideas*. We can have good ideas that help people and will even be successful, but if we are not on track with God's plan we can get side tracked. The enemy likes to get us side tracked from God's plan. The only way to know that an idea is from

God is to look at the source of the idea. God will always be the source of His idea. His ideas come from the Holy Spirit and they are impossible to complete without Him. Also He will always supply the resources to carry out His ideas.

I went to a prophetic conference this weekend and noticed that quite a few people were getting prophetic confirmations to start businesses. The prophetic is a powerful tool. Remember, a prophetic word is God speaking to us *through* a human vessel. Prophecy is a very important key in determining a God idea from a good idea. I would like to add that the business ideas I speak about in this book are just that: "God ideas". They are in the idea/start-up stage as I write this book. I am prophetically speaking these *God ideas* into existence within the pages of this book. It should be an interesting adventure. Come join the fun!

Chapter 1
RELATIONSHIPS

God always has our best interest at heart. When it comes to relationships, there are *God* relationships and there are manmade relationships. We think, in this world that a man or woman can help us get to where we are going. I believe this is true, but only through relationships that are *God* relationships.

For instance, my wife and I are a great example of a woman and man that is based upon God relationships. There are many people who are married or will get married whose marriages might appear to be a *good* idea. If it is not a *God* idea then some kind of failure is inevitable. I once was engaged to someone that I thought was a *God* idea, but in reality it was a good idea. I was getting older and it was harder to find someone that was not already married or did not have kids. Since this was my main criteria, I thought I had found the woman God had for me. Even if you have a list of what you are looking for in a mate, God knows what you need better than you do. She matched several items on my list that made me believe she was the one for me. I was using my soul as the source, instead of my spirit. I am a person that would never give up on any situation. But after many years of disappointment and heartache, I began to realize that she was indeed a *good* idea instead of a *God* idea. I am very thankful that I did not marry this woman. It would have been a *huge* mistake.

In chapter 15:2-6 "But Abram said, "Lord God, what will You give me, seeing I go childless, and the heir of my house is Eliezer of Damascus?" Then Abram said, "Look, You have given me no offspring; indeed one born in my house is my heir!" And behold the word of the Lord came to him, saying, "This one shall not be your heir, but one who will come from your own body shall be your heir." Then He brought him outside and said, "Look now toward heaven, and count the stars if you are able to number them." And He said to him, "So shall your descendants be." And he believed in the Lord, and He accounted it to him for righteousness. And then in chapter 16:2,5 "So Sarai said to Abraham, "See now, the Lord has restrained me from bearing children. Please, go in to my maid; perhaps I shall obtain children by her." And Abram heeded the voice of Sarai." In verse 5 "Then

Sarai said to Abram, "My wrong be upon you! I gave my maid into your embrace; and when she saw that she had conceived, I became despised in her eyes. The Lord judge between you and me." In these scriptures we see how God gave Abram His idea of an heir but Sarai had a good idea of her own. It didn't take long for her to realize that her good idea was not what God had in mind for an heir. We have to trust God with His ideas. He does things different than we do. He is also not in any kind of hurry. Time is not an issue with God. Timing is another key.

I had received a prophetic word from two different sources that I would marry a blonde woman. I didn't pay much attention because I had my eyes set on a brunette. God knew in my heart, even when I didn't know, what kind of woman I needed to marry. After several years had passed, I met my wife. She is definitely a *God* idea. She met my criteria of having no kids and never having been married, but the rest of her characteristics, I would not have envisioned being in my "ideal" wife. My Heavenly Father knows the destiny of my life because He created me. So He knows the characteristics of the woman I need to marry in order for us to fulfill our destiny together. My wife and I are complete opposites of each other. She is fun and outgoing. I am more reserved and laidback. I am very conservative in the financial area. She has a great eye for high end items. It takes the Holy Spirit for us to come together as one. Neither one of us can do this through our own power. This is a "*God* idea" relationship.

Besides my wife, I have other personal and business relationships that are from God. I am business partners with two ideal God friends. My best friend and best man at my wedding is a relationship God put together. I had not seen him in many years. Then, all of a sudden I ran into him at the racetrack and then at a St. Louis Rams football game. I really felt in my spirit that God was definitely trying to get us together. He knew the future destiny for both of us. Today we are business partners and best friends. The Holy Spirit put that relationship together.

Now let's look at some Bible scriptures to get a better understanding of a *God* idea. In Genesis chapter 24 Abraham wants to find a bride for his son Isaac. Abraham does not want his son to marry a Canaanite woman. Abraham wants him to marry a woman from his own country which is Haran to maintain the purity of the bloodline. In verse 7 he says, "The Lord God of heaven, who took me from my father's house and from the land of my family, and who spoke to me and swore to me, saying, 'To your descendants I give this land,' He will send his angel before you, and you shall take a wife for my son from there." So Abraham sends his servant to the city of Nahor. In Genesis chapter 24:11-19 "And he made his camels kneel down outside the city by a well of water at evening time, the time when women go out to draw water. Then he said, "O Lord God of my master Abraham, please give me success this day, and show kindness to my master Abraham. "Behold, here I stand by the well of water, and the daughters of the men of the city are coming out to draw water. "Now let it be that the young woman to whom I say, "Please let down your pitcher that I may drink and she says, "Drink and I will also give your camels a drink-let her be the one You have appointed for Your servant Isaac. And by this I will know that You have shown kindness to my master." And it happened, before he had finished speaking, that behold Rebekah, who was born to Bethel, son of Milcah, the wife of Nahor, Abraham's brother came out with her pitcher on her shoulder. Now the young woman was very beautiful to behold, a virgin; no man had known her. And she went down to the well, filled her pitcher, and came up. And the servant ran to meet her and said, "Please let me drink a little water from your pitcher." So she said, "Drink my lord." Then she quickly let her pitcher down to her hand, and gave him a drink. And when she had finished giving him a drink, she said, "I will draw water for your camels also, until they have finished drinking." And then in verse 21-27 "And the man, wondering at her, remained silent so as to know whether the Lord had made his journey prosperous or not. So it was, when the camels had finished drinking, that the man took a golden nose ring weighing half a shekel, and two bracelets for her wrists weighing ten shekels of gold and said, "Whose daughter are you? Tell me, please, is there room in your father's house for us to lodge?" So she said, "I am the daughter of Bethuel, Milcah's son, whom she bore to Nahor." Moreover she said to him, "We have both straw and feed enough, and room to lodge." Then the man bowed down his head and worshiped the Lord. And he said, "Blessed be the Lord God of my master Abraham, who has not forsaken His mercy and His truth toward my master. As for me, being on the way, the Lord led me to the house of my master's brethren."

As you can clearly see in these scriptures, this is a *God* idea from the very beginning. God's ideas may not be practical to us. One important part of a *God* idea is that you need to have faith in His idea. Because we are children of the most high God, He cares deeply about our lives. He is our heavenly Father and He does know what He is doing. This is difficult for us to understand and that is where our faith comes in to the picture. We must put our trust in something we cannot see. "For we walk by faith, not by sight." (In 2 Corinthians 5:7)

Chapter 2
BUSINESS

A business always starts from an idea. I have had many business ideas over the years. My first business was selling drugs. I have a business anointing but this is not what God had in mind. At the time it seemed like a good idea. I was making good money. I remember coming home and having more money in my pocket than when I had left the house because I would go to parties and sell drugs. I had strange people knocking on my parent's front door, looking for me. I was still working a full time job, too. Since I didn't need to spend any of my paycheck I had a good deal of money in the bank. I had someone selling the drugs for me, beside myself. In this business, there is no one you can trust. This individual stole all the drugs from my "secret" hiding place. I now had a serious problem, because I had been advanced this marijuana. That meant that I still needed to pay for it. I was so glad

I had saved some money. This was the end of this business. I had an opportunity to harm the individual that stole the drugs from me, but I decided I did not want to be a drug dealer for the rest of my life. I would also like to say that I had a praying grandma that got me out of this business. She lives with Jesus now but I would like to personally thank her for praying me out of harm's way. This was not a *God* idea. This was not even a *good* idea. This was a **bad** idea that Satan could have used to alter my destiny forever.

The next business I had was cutting grass. This business, actually, fell in my lap. Some friends of mine had some lawns and didn't want to cut them anymore. I took over the lawns, and added some more to the business. It was a great part time business and it made money. This business finally ended when I blew the motor up in my car. It was my own fault that the motor blew up. I was out in the world and more focused on having fun than being responsible. This car was the vehicle I was using to pull the equipment trailer. I *believe* this was a *good* idea. Not a *God* idea.

Manufacturing is where I have most of my experience, even though I have a Finance degree. After I graduated from Texas Tech in 1998, I went to work for my parents. They had started a filling company called Benton Drumming. We filled 55 gallons drums with oil additives. I was so excited about this business. I jumped in with both feet. I thought this was my ticket to riches. After a lot of hard work and disappointments, the business closed in 2004. I now had to figure out what to do next. I believed this company was a *God* idea and that we would be very successful. I can say it was a *good* idea but God had other plans. I am grateful for all of the experience that I acquired while working at Benton Drumming. I learned a lot at this company. I am able to use my acquired experiences in current and future opportunities.

Retail is another business that I thought was a *God* idea. My brother and I started a car stereo business. I started this business out of passion for car stereos. I thought I could do it better and cheaper than other stores already in the business. The problem with starting a business from the soul instead of the Spirit is the difference between failure and success. I did very little research before we started this business. I have a finance degree. I was being led by my emotions instead of basic business knowledge. I did not do my due diligence before opening up the store. I didn't even check to see if the rent I was paying was market value. I just said, "Where do I sign?" I listened to what other people were saying to me, instead of checking out facts for myself. We tried this business two different times in two different locations and were unsuccessful both times.

I didn't pray about starting this car stereo business. The Holy Spirit must be involved in our decision making process. I never even asked my brother if he really wanted to be in the business. I just assumed he would want to do it. We had no business plan. We had no money in reserve. The day we opened it was depending on sales to survive. This put a lot of unnecessary pressure on us from the very beginning. It made our working relationship very stressful.

Looking back, this retail business has high overhead (rent, inventory, marketing, etc.). The profit margins are thin. The car stereo market is saturated. It is a manufacturer driven business. This was not a *good* business to be in, in the first place. This was not a *God* idea.

Through a series of events, I found myself selling my single family home and buying a duplex in a lower income area. I had a Hispanic family renting from me next door. The *God* idea was to find them a home, rehab it and sell the home to them contract for deed. Over the next five and half to six years I bought and sold six homes to Hispanic families. I learned a lot through this process and by the end of the six years it became a very profitable business. My last house I made the most money and did the least amount of work. Sometimes it takes a while to see the real *God* idea. I would also like to mention that my wife and I are currently living off of the income that comes in from these properties. So God knew back then that we would both lose our jobs and need a source of income through our transition period. God is always thinking ahead.

As I mentioned earlier, I have a real estate business that buys and sells property. I decided it would be a *good* idea to start managing property. I have a friend that needed tenants for his duplex. We signed a property management agreement. We agreed upon 7% management fee. I had to work very hard for very little money. I should have prayed about this new opportunity before I jumped into it. I did learn a lot but, this was not a *God* idea. Another real estate related opportunity came along after this property management idea. The new idea was to get into general contracting. This good idea didn't turn out any better than the property management idea. I was being led by the "thought" of it being a *good* idea instead of being led by the Holy Spirit. A "thought" is usually from the soul. Praying will reveal the truth.

Now I would like to share a *God* idea. My brother is a very smart person. He loves electronics. This is the reason he liked the car stereo business. He took a product that was available and made some minor "tweaks" to it. Now we can all unlock and lock our car doors with our phones. He has started a company called Mobile Enhancement Specialist. Go to www.bluetoothkeyless.info to check out his product. I have been with him to several trade shows and potential customers love the product. This is a product that can be made with a small amount of start-up capital. It has unlimited potential because there are so many cars on the road around the world. The best part is that no one else is making this product. The overhead cost is low and the profit margins are high. It did not cost a lot to start the business. He did not take any outside investment money. He also has no start-up debt. He has retained 100% of the company. This is a *God* idea.

    I would like to share with you about another business idea that came from God. Not long after I had been with my brother at a couple trade shows, God began to speak to me about getting together with two other friends of mine and praying about new business ideas. We met a few Saturdays in March of 2013 and came up with an idea to create an all-natural energy drink. Within only a few months we had a formula. In the beverage industry, it can take years to come up with a formula. So this was great to see such amazing progress so quickly. Then one of the guys realized he had gotten a prophetic word about a product similar to what we had created. The following is the prophetic word: "I see you getting a product that you and a few guys will put together, what it is going to cause is a detox energy increasing, whatever people are lacking it's going to change things around, no chemicals in it, it's going to be natural stuff. It's going to be something that you and a few guys are going to put together and pray over. It's not going to be cheap and it's not going to be expensive. It's going to be very successful. I see you getting a lot of people on this stuff." We knew for sure this was a *God* idea when we read this prophecy. Today, we have two flavors of Ju'bilee Tea that is all-natural and will be hitting the market sometime in the near future. Go to www.drinkjubilee.com to find out more information. We may not always have a prophetic word to confirm an idea but we can ask God to confirm His idea. Another key to a *God* idea is having the resources to carry out the vision. God always provides provision for His vision.

In the scriptures, Joseph was able to interpret the dream that the Pharaoh of Egypt had. This dream or idea came from God. Joseph was able to interpret the dream for the Pharaoh. This really was a business idea from God. In Genesis 41:49 "Joseph gathered very much grain, as the sand of the sea, until he stopped counting, for it was immeasurable." Then in Genesis 41:56-57 "The famine was over all the face of the earth and Joseph opened all the storehouses and sold to the Egyptians. And the famine became severe in the land of Egypt. So all countries came to Joseph in Egypt to buy grain, because the famine was severe in all lands." This is an amazing *God* idea. There are seven years of plenty, so Joseph stores it up. Then, when the seven years of famine come upon the lands, he is the only one with grain. That means everyone had to buy from Joseph or starve to death. This *God* idea produced an enormous profit for Joseph and Egypt. God is all about business ideas. If we will co-labor with Him, the possibilities are limitless.

An amazing opportunity has occurred while writing this book. It is like I'm walking out this book in *real* time. I was drinking a fountain soda one day in a plastic cup and the sweat kept running down the side of it. I thought there has to be something to take care of this problem. To my surprise, there is not a product out there to keep your plastic fountain soda cup cold. They exist for other cups, but not plastic fountain soda cups. Later that night I began experimenting with a solution to this problem. That night God gave me a proto-type design for a fountain cup cooler that wraps around a plastic fountain cup. I have since refined it a few times.

I had my good friend Tim at Designland make me a very cool logo. I found a manufacturing company overseas to make the koozie for me. I am currently marketing this product to large convenient store chains in the Midwest. It will also be available for purchase online @ www.fountainfriendkooziekompany.com. I believe this is a *God* idea. It is amazing to see what God is doing through me as I write this book. Always keep in mind that ideas need to be walked out in real life. A *God idea* doesn't do any good staying inside your head. I encourage everyone to walk out their *God ideas*.

Chapter 3

INVESTING

I have invested in many *good* ideas. I put my money in some penny stocks that I thought was a *good* idea. Penny stocks are stocks that sell for less than a dollar per share. These stocks are very high risk. I had this particular penny stock that I thought lined up with a prophetic word. I believed in my heart that it would go to a dollar per share. I bought about a $1000 worth of this stock. The stock went up to approximately $10,000. I didn't sell it because I believed it would go even higher. Then the next day it dropped like a rock. Next time I will sell when I have a profit. I did just that with the same stock and made $1000. That is not the same as $10,000 but at least I was learning from my previous mistake.

Another time I bought a different penny stock with my retirement account. I believed this stock was going to take off as well. I think by the time I sold my shares in this company, my retirement account was down $8000-

$9000. I have to *admit* that I was not asking the Holy Spirit for guidance with these stock picks. This was a hard lesson to learn and was not a *God* idea.

I did buy a stock that was a *God* idea. My parents and I follow Kim Clement the Prophet. He gave a prophetic word about Ford Motor Company, that the company would not take a government bailout and would recover from the losses. My parents had already started buying the stock. I was busy with other things and didn't think much of it at the time. Then, I was watching a Kim Clement broadcast and he began talking about Ford again. All of a sudden, the Holy Spirit came over me like a rushing wind. It was like the anointing was covering my entire body. I knew right then that this investment was a *God* idea. I began using any money I could get my hands on to buy Ford stock. I even used credit cards for cash advances to buy stock. After about a year or so, I sold the stock and made approximately $50,000 gross profit. This was the most money I had ever made at one time off of any investment. I did very little work to acquire this money. You see *God* ideas pay off really well and usually do not require much work on our part. Another key to a *God* idea is obedience. What if I didn't listen to the Holy Spirit when he was trying to get my attention? I would have lost out on a *God* idea to make some money.

I decided to invest in a window tinting business. I knew there was good money in window tinting businesses. I had done some training in the business before so I was familiar with how it worked. I was not a good window tinter but had the knowledge to manage. I did some due diligence about the potential partner. Also there was an operating agreement that we both signed. It seemed like a small risk for a big potential reward. So I went through with the $2000 investment. It only took a few months for the business to fold up and the investment was gone. Another key to a *God* idea is prayer. The Holy Spirit is our helper. We need to use him. I did not pray about this investment before I wrote the check. I had to learn that lesson the hard way. Please pray before you invest and choose the right business partners.

I invested in a piece of property that I bought at a tax auction. A tax auction is when the taxes have not been paid for 3 years, so the county auctions off the property to the highest bidder. One problem with these auctions is that we are not legally able to inspect the property. This can be a dangerous situation. I went to look around the outside of the property and noticed some gold dust on a car cover. Gold dust is a supernatural sign from Heaven. I immediately thought this property was fine. I bought the house at the auction. Once inside I realized that the roof had been leaking in the kitchen for many years. It was so bad we had to take down one exterior wall and replace it. Then we had to replace the entire roof over the kitchen. As I am writing this book the house is still not finished. I have a lot of time and money invested in this project. It is difficult for me to say if this is a *God* idea or a *good* idea that I came up with myself. I am trusting God to either sell the house "as is" or find a way to finish it and sell it for a profit. Another key is trust. I just remembered that I received a very large insurance check for this property from a hail storm. I believe that I received all of my investment back. You see, God can bail us out of our own mistakes.

The Holy Spirit reminded me, the next day, after writing the above paragraph that I did have an opportunity to sell this house right after I purchased it. I declined the potential buyers offer. So God actually gave me an opportunity to make a profit on this investment. I wanted to rehab the house and sell it like I had done with the others. God does not do things the same all the time. He likes to change things up. I didn't follow His lead. I wanted to do it *my* way.

Let's go to the scriptures to get more insight. In Genesis chapter 29 Jacob meets Rachel. He marries Leah and Rachel. Laban had deceived Jacob many times. Jacob is ready to leave and go to his country. He wants his wages for all the time invested in Laban's flock. So Laban and Jacob make an agreement that all the speckled and spotted sheep and goats would be Jacob's. In Genesis 30:35-39 "So he removed that day the male goats that were speckled and spotted, all the female goats that were speckled and spotted, every one that had some white in it, and all the brown ones among the lambs, and gave them into the hands of his sons. Then he put three days' journey between himself and Jacob, and Jacob fed the rest of Laban's flocks. Now Jacob took for himself rods of green poplar and of the almond and chestnut trees, peeled white strips in them and exposed the white which was in the rods. And the rods which he had peeled, he set before the flocks in the gutters, in the watering troughs where the flocks came to drink, so that they should conceive when they came to drink. So the flocks conceived before the rods and the flocks brought forth streaked, speckled, and spotted." This was a *God idea* that Jacob received in a dream. In Genesis 31:11-12 "Then the Angel of God spoke to me in a dream, saying, "Jacob." And I said, "Here I am." And He said, "Lift up your eyes now and see, all the rams which leap on the flocks are streaked, speckled, and gray-spotted; for I have seen all that Laban is doing to you." Jacob's investment has just paid off by having faith and trusting in *God's idea*.

Chapter 4
MINISTRY

I think we all have a *good* idea when it comes to ministry. We want to help people and further the Kingdom of God. The challenging part for me is to see that God wants to use me for more than my natural gifts. I enjoy helping people with their finances. I enjoy teaching finances to the men and women of God. I have a Finance degree and this is a natural gift God has given me.

I know that God has called me to do much more than teach finances. He also wants me to prophecy to the body of Christ. This requires faith, spending a lot of time in prayer, and relying on the supernatural gifts of heaven. This is a major challenge for me. This will require me to step out of my comfort zone. Writing books has definitely gotten me out of my comfort zone. I'm not a good salesman so it is difficult for me to sell myself. This does relate to prophesying to people because it requires me to be confident in God and trust the Holy Spirit. We all have supernatural gifts from God that are *God* ideas. He created us so He knows the gifts that are in us. The Holy Spirit is our helper to bring these gifts out.

Another gift that I have discovered through the help of the Holy Spirit is writing books. This is a ministry that can reach millions of people. I do not have a natural gift of writing. I decided to step out of my comfort zone and rely on the Holy Spirit to help me. I can honestly say, "The Holy Spirit has been amazing". He is giving me so much help. Just today He gave me a title for the next book and I have not even finished this one yet. I believe I have found a well for writing books. I intend to write as many books as possible during this season of my life. The Holy Spirit is so good to me. I feel as though we are partners working together on a common goal. God has His idea of ministry for us to do and we have our own desires as well. We cannot do **His ideas** without the Holy Spirit. We can do **our ideas** but it comes from the soul not the spirit.

In John chapter 14:12-18 "Most assuredly, I say to you, he who believes in Me, the works that I do he will do also; and greater works than these he will do, because I go to my Father. And whatever you ask in My name, that I will do, that the Father may be glorified in the Son. If you ask anything in My name, I will do it. If you love Me, keep my commandments. And I will pray the Father, and He will give you another Helper, that He may abide with you forever- the Spirit of truth, whom the world cannot receive, because it neither sees Him nor knows Him; but you know Him, for He dwells with you and will be in you. I will not leave you orphans; I will come to you." Also in John chapter 15:26-27 "But when the Helper comes, whom I shall send to you from the Father, the Spirit of truth who proceeds from the Father, He will testify of Me. And you also will bear witness, because you have been with Me from the beginning."

God is telling us that if we will love Him, trust in Him and follow His commandments, that He will in return send a Helper to strengthen us in our time of need. God's whole plan is for us to work together with the Helper. He does not expect us to do His ideas by ourself. Trying to do *God's* idea by ourselves is man's idea. Another problem with man (soul) trying to do God's work is that we will mess up His plan for us. In ministry we tend to be pulled in a certain direction by our soul. We believe that what we are doing is of God. Remember the Pharisees thought they were doing God's work by killing Jesus. Deception is a powerful tool that the enemy uses to get us to believe what we are doing is the plan that God has for us. Ask yourself: *who is the source of the ministry.* God is the source of ministry and no ministry can be fulfilled without the help of the Creator.

Chapter 5
SOUL

This is the most difficult part: determining if the idea we receive is from the soul or spirit. As you may have noticed in the beginning of this book, I used examples of my life that were *God* ideas and *good* ideas. This is a process that we all go through each day in our lives. We learn from this process and in future opportunities become more aware of the source of the idea. The key is to determine if the idea came from your soul/flesh or from your soul/spirit. There is no magic formula to determine the source of the idea. As we go through the process of learning how to hear God, each day we get closer to determining His voice.

For me the soul/flesh ideas always **sound** like a good idea. In other words, managing property sounded in my *mind* like a good idea. So the source of this idea didn't come from my soul/spirit. This idea came from my mind or soul/flesh. The mind can imagine all kinds of different things. God gave us this imagination. Our imagination is a very powerful tool, but the flesh can also corrupt that God given imagination. We have to keep our focus on the One who gives us the ideas. In 2 Corinthians 10:3-6 "For though we walk in the flesh, we do not war according to the flesh. For the weapons of our warfare are not carnal but mighty in God for pulling down strongholds, casting down arguments and every high thing that exalts itself against the knowledge of God, bringing every thought into captivity to the obedience of Christ, and being ready to punish all disobedience when your obedience is fulfilled." This scripture is intended for spiritual warfare. Our imagination is a constant battle ground between spirit and flesh. God is giving us a key in this battle. If a thought (idea) is exalting itself against God, then it's not from God. He is also letting us know that we are to have the spirit control our imagination, not our flesh. This is a daily process we all go through. The more we are able to learn from this process, the more we are able to understand if an idea is from the spirit or from the flesh.

Emotions can play a very important part in the origin of an idea. This is one of my personal struggles. As I am sure you can see from some of my personal examples in the beginning of the book, I have made decisions based upon a good feeling. The flesh will convince you that this is a good idea because it feels good or it sounds good. Emotions can lead us down the wrong path but I believe passion can guide us down the right path. We should all be passionate about our Heavenly Father. We should pursue Him with the utmost passion. He wants to do the same thing with us. The problem is that we can't get our flesh out of the way. The flesh always wants to do something else. Our Spirit wants to pursue the Holy Spirit. He is our Counselor in every area of our lives, including when it comes to ideas. He can make things happen that you never thought possible. This is why it is so important to co-labor with Christ. If you have an idea that you are very passionate about then it was probably put there by the Holy Spirit. The best way to find out is to just ask Him. This is where our relationship with the Holy Spirit must be strong. Remember He is here to help us.

In John 14:15-17 "If you love Me, keep My commandments. And I will pray the Father, and He will give you another Helper, that He may abide with you forever- the Spirit of truth, whom the world cannot receive, because it neither sees Him, nor knows Him; but you know Him, for He dwells with you and will be in you." This scripture gives us some keys to help us understand soul/spirit: First we have to keep His commandments, and then He will pray to the Father for us and give us a Helper which is the Holy Spirit/"Spirit of truth". The Spirit of truth which dwells inside of us will guide us to what is the truth. A *God idea* is the truth. A good idea is a fact. It might be a fact that an idea will work but the **truth** of an idea will be successful because we are co-laboring with Heaven. You see, heaven already knows the outcome of this idea before we ever get started on implementing it into the world. This is an amazing revelation if you can grasp it. Imagine your success rate!

Chapter 6
SPIRIT

This is the most difficult part of the book for me to write about: knowing when it is the Holy Spirit and not our soul. I first have to say that I don't understand how or why God does things. It is difficult for our human minds to understand. I do know that He loves us because He sent His only **Son** to die for *our* sins. Based upon this knowing, I know that He has my best interest at heart at all times. So we have to decide whether or not to trust in Him. This is always easier to talk or write about than to **live** it out.

For instance, I am listening to the Holy Spirit as I write this book. I stopped for a moment to read the previous chapter. I began to question if this is what I should be saying. This is my soul trying to make sure that everything I am writing makes sense. God does not always make sense to our natural minds. We have to learn to get our natural minds out of the way. Then, God can speak directly to our spirit. This is the relationship that He desires to have with us.

I believe that personal experience is the best teacher. I am going to share a recent experience that I had. My wife and I have believed for a certain house. We drive by the house periodically to prophetically call it into existence. The house has been for sale for a few years. We drove by to see it and noticed that the "for sale" sign was missing out of the yard and the porch lights were on. I immediately, out of my *soul* not my *spirit* assumed someone had bought the house. I used my natural logic and came to the conclusion someone had purchased the home and would be moving into it. I did not even think about what God might have in store for us.

I went home that night and had to repent to God. I was allowing my soul/flesh to interpret what was going on with the house. I was not supporting my wife who had all the faith in the world to believe that this house is **still** ours. I was so disappointed with myself. We did find out the house has been sold but that does not mean it is not ours. God does things completely different than how we think He will do them. An investor may have bought the house. I don't really know what God is up to with this property and that is what is driving my flesh crazy. God is using this situation to show me I still have some work to do in this department. This is a process that requires: time, discipline, failure, patience, choices and love. I have failed many times in the battle of soul vs. spirit, but I keep getting up and trying again. God is so patient with us that He will give us many opportunities to try something again. His love is unconditional. Our choices determine the direction we go in life. He will discipline us and love us at the same time. For the Creator of the universe, time is nothing to Him.

I am determined to understand the difference between my soul and spirit. I believe everyone has a *God idea* inside of them just waiting to come out into the world. This is my passion, to see the body of Christ, bring forth the *God ideas* that He planted inside each and every person on this planet. My prayer is that every person that reads this book will be inspired to search within their spirit for *God ideas*.

Chapter 7
PROPHECY

Prophecy is a very important part of my life. I mention prophecy quite a bit in this book. Prophecy is important because it gives us a glance at our future. A prophetic word can sustain us during the difficult times in our life. It can literally be our life line to the future.

There are several misconceptions about prophecy. One misconception is that prophecy is unconditional. The truth is we have to do *our* part in the prophecy before God can do *His* part. For example, I received numerous prophetic words about writing a book and that it would be successful. I had to write the book first before God can make it successful. Also we can think a prophetic word means something when God is thinking of something else. I will use my first book as an example; God said, "It would be **successful**". Now **my**

idea of "successful" and **God's idea** of "successful" can be two entirely different thoughts.

Prophecy is to be a guide for us. If we get a prophetic word from a Prophet or prophetic person, we have to *pray out* that word. We still have to seek God for interpretation and divine revelation. God can give us an *idea* and we can miss our opportunity if we are not seeking Him.

Timing is everything in a prophetic word. I did some writing while I was employed at my job. Once I was let go from that job I was able to finish my first book. Then a writing well of anointing opened up for me. This is my second book and it is going very quickly. God has given me a title for my third book. My point to all this is that it had to be the right timing for all this to happen. It all started with me losing my job. I knew that losing my job was a *God* idea. They let me go for a very minor reason. I also knew from prophetic words that God had other plans for my life instead of working in a factory. What I did not know was that I would enter into this season of writing books.

Prophecy can be a very powerful tool. The problems with prophecy is that most people don't understand it, don't know how to receive it, and most importantly, don't know how to fulfill it. I would suggest reading Dr.

Bill Hamon's book "Prophets and Personal Prophecy" for a more in depth look at this subject.

I would like to go to the scriptures and see what it has to say about prophecy; In 1 Corinthians 14:1-5 "Pursue love, and desire spiritual gifts, but especially that you may prophesy. For he who speaks in a tongue does not speak to men but to God, for no one understands him; however, in the spirit he speaks mysteries. But he who prophesies speaks edification and exhortation and comfort to men. He who speaks in tongue edifies himself, but he who prophesies edifies the church. I wish you all spoke with tongues, but even more that you prophesied; for he who prophesies is greater than he who speaks with tongues, unless indeed he interprets, that the church may receive edification."

These scriptures indicate how important it is to prophesy. God has given us all a gift of prophesy. We just have it in different levels. In 1 Corinthians 14:31 "For you can all prophesy one by one, that all may learn and all may be encouraged." We need to be able to prophecy to ourselves as well as to others.

Another important part of using prophecy as a guide or confirmation on a *God idea* is to make sure the prophetic voice is from God. The source of the prophetic voice that you are listening to needs to come from Heaven. I have seen and heard too many prophetic voices coming from the man himself (his soul). This makes it very difficult to know if the prophetic word is accurate. I encourage everyone to seek out seasoned men and women of God to help steer you in the right direction. The church does not use the prophetic voice because of this very reason; the church believes that the prophetic voice is not of God. I believe God and the prophetic voice has gotten a misrepresentation in this matter. There *are* men and women of God who prophesy from their spirit and not their soul. We as a church just need to *seek* those prophetic voices out. God wants us to give direction to His people through the prophetic voice. In 2 Peter 1:16-21 "For we did not follow cunningly devised fables when we made known to you the power and coming of our Lord Jesus Christ, but were eyewitnesses of His majesty. For He received from God the Father honor and glory when such a voice came to Him from the Excellent Glory: "This is My beloved Son, in whom I am well pleased." And we heard this voice which came from heaven when we were with Him on the holy mountain. And so we have the prophetic word confirmed, which you do well to heed as a light that shines in a dark place, until the day dawns and the morning star rises in your hearts; knowing this first, that no prophecy of Scripture is of any private interpretation, for prophecy never came by the will of man, but holy men of God spoke as they were moved by the Holy Spirit."

Chapter 8
DIVINE COUNCIL

The main reason for writing this book is to help people with their *God* ideas. I believe there are millions of people out there with *God* ideas. The problem with some people and their ideas is they don't know what to do with them. The world has reality shows with entrepreneurs pitching ideas to investors. I don't believe some of these investors have the entrepreneur's best interest at heart.

The church today has many ideas. They just need people they can trust to help them fulfill the idea God gave them. Some people are afraid that their idea will be stolen from them. Other people lack the experience to move the idea forward. Whatever the problem may be, I have a solution to help people fulfill their destiny. I have set up a website: www.igotgodidea.com. This will be a community of kingdom counselors. Here, a person can ask questions and get answers from trustworthy people. Every counselor is a man or woman of God that will be able to help you bring your *God idea* into reality. I believe the body of Christ needs to work together and bring these *God ideas* to market.

We have to remember that we all have strengths and weaknesses. If we can set our differences aside and team up with people who have the strengths we need, then the potential is unlimited. In the world they would call this an incubator for start-ups. This community of counselors is the Kingdom way for start-ups. The Kingdom way will see the value in helping other people succeed and not how much money they can make from the person's idea.

God is waiting on the church to rise up and take its place in the market place. There are so many *dead ideas* in the church; ideas that came from God but no one did anything with it. Then the world comes along and takes the *God idea* and turns it into a billion dollar business for the world. I am personally sick and tired of seeing this happen. There are a lot of Bill Gates and Mark Zuckerberg out there for the Kingdom of God. Most of these people just need some trustworthy council. There are also many people in the body of Christ who have yet to unlock their *God ideas*.

Fear and failure are two reasons many people will not move forward on a *God idea*. I have had many experiences throughout the years of fear and failure. We have to fail before we can succeed. God will give us the strength we need to endure through these times. It is also very important to surround yourself with positive influential people. This is where the community of counselors comes into our lives. This is a place where people can get feedback and support for their *God ideas*. We all need someone to help us get to our destiny. I believe this community of counselors can be an important part of the future market place for believers. God is raising up a new breed of believers in this hour.

Integrity will be a vital part of this community of counselors. God is looking for a group of people who will carry out His plans to bring His Kingdom from heaven to earth. I believe we are in a time of extreme abundance. We have to stay focused on God during these times. It will be very helpful to have counselors to help us stay focused on the kingdom. It is very easy to get off track when the abundance begins to flow. Always remember Who the source of the abundance is.

Wisdom is knowledge. Many people in the body of Christ believe that they know a lot and do not need anyone's help. In Proverbs 29:3 "Whoever loves wisdom makes his father rejoice, but a companion of harlots wastes his wealth." In other words it is wise to get advice from someone that is knowledgeable in that area. Otherwise we will just be wasting our money. That is why I'm putting up this website: www.igotgodidea.com. This website will have wise council for people to ask questions and get answers before they spend their money. I am investing into the Body of Christ. I believe this is a time of great creativity. We just have to unlock it and be willing to work together. The Body of Christ is like a corporation. A corporation has a CEO, Board of Directors, shareholders, employees, managers, and customers. Everyone needs everyone else. The world understands this concept, its time the church take hold of this as well.

In Proverbs 24:3-7 "Through wisdom a house is built, and by understanding it is established; by knowledge the rooms are filled with all precious and pleasant riches. A wise man is strong, yes, a man of knowledge increases strength; For by wise council you will wage your own war, and in a multitude of counselors there is safety. Wisdom is too lofty for a fool; he does not open his mouth in the gate."

In Proverbs 11:14 "Where there is no counsel, the people fall; but in the multitude of counselors there is safety." Also in Proverbs 1:24-31 "Because I have called and you refused, I have stretched out my hand and no one regarded, because you disdained all my counsel, and would have none of my rebuke, I also will laugh at your calamity; I will mock when your terror comes, when your terror comes like a storm, and your destruction comes like a whirlwind, when distress and anguish come upon you. Then they will call on me, but I will not answer; they will seek me diligently, but they will not find me. Because they hated knowledge and did not choose the fear of the Lord, they would have none of my counsel and despised my every rebuke. Therefore they shall eat the fruit of their own way, and be filled to the full with their own fancies."

Remember there is no secret formula to figure out if it is a *God idea* or a *good idea*. God wants us to get council from Him. He also wants us to listen to Him. If we try to do things on our own it will not turn out good. For some reason, we always like to learn the hard way. My prayer is that the Body of Christ will read this book and begin to see that all believers are on the same team. We need to work together in every area but I am concentrating on the business/marketplace area. If we can set aside our differences and realize we all need some type of council/help then we can take back the marketplace for our Lord and Savior, Jesus Christ. Let's take the marketplace by **FORCE!!!**

God Idea or Good Idea Evaluation Sheet

This evaluation sheet is a guide. This is to help you think about your idea. If you would like a more in-depth evaluation visit: www.igotgodidea.com. There you can submit your entire idea and receive Godly council.

1. Origin of the idea? Example; Holy Spirit, soul, emotions, etc.

2. Does it help people? Who gains?

3. Does it require faith to accomplish?

4. Do you need to trust God to fulfill idea?

5. Is He asking you to step out of your comfort zone?

6. Is God requiring more obedience?

7. Can you do it without God?

8. Do you have provision for the vision?

9. Any prophetic insight?

10. Have you prayed about the idea?

Contact the Author
Kevin L. Cann

Kingdom Management & Investments, LLC

Email:

kevincann@kingdommanagement101.com

Website:
www.kingdommanagement101.com

Website: www.igotgodidea.com

OTHER BOOKS AVAILABLE

By Kevin Cann

Who Is Your $ource

Sunday $pending Instead of Sunday Giving

By Mark Krenning

More of Him, Less of Me

Available Everywhere Books Are Sold

www.ingramcontent.com/pod-product-compliance
Lightning Source LLC
Chambersburg PA
CBHW072113290426
44110CB00014B/1898